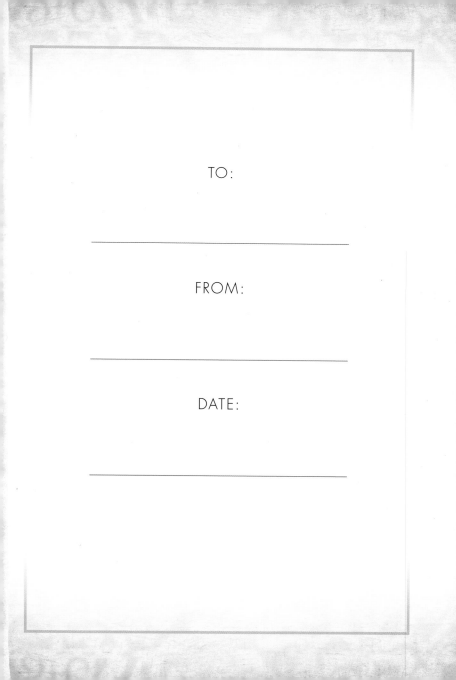

TO:

_____

FROM:

_____

DATE:

_____

Finding God's BLESSINGS in BROKENNESS

HOW PAIN REVEALS HIS DEEPEST LOVE

CHARLES F. STANLEY

ZONDERVAN®

To the members of First Baptist Church of Atlanta, who faithfully supported me in my times of brokenness.

CONTENTS

CHAPTER 1

BROKEN AND BLESSED?

Broken.

Broken.
Blessed.

The two words don't seem to go together.

We all know what it means to be broken, to be shattered, to feel as if our entire world has fallen apart or perhaps been blown apart. We all have times in our lives when we don't want to raise our heads off the pillow and when we are certain the tears will never stop flowing. We feel a void that cannot be filled, a sorrow that cannot be comforted, a wound for which there seems no balm.

Nothing feels blessed about being broken. In fact, certain circumstances in life hurt so intensely that we think we will never heal. But blessing can come in the wake of our being broken.

And this blessing is richest when we not only let ourselves fully experience the brokenness but also wrestle with God over why he allowed us to be broken. When we cooperate with God as he does his refining and transformational work in us, his blessing will follow our brokenness.

RUNNING FROM OR FACING THE PAIN?

As we journey through this life—through the easy times and the painful times—God is fashioning us into people who are like his Son, Jesus. That means God is in the process of *changing* what we desire far more than he is in the process of *giving* us what we desire.

Part of being like Jesus is being willing to do whatever God desires: "Not my will, but yours be done" (Luke 22:42).

Now, if I asked you, "Do you really want God's best for your life?" I feel confident that you would say, "Yes, of course!"

But if I asked you, "Are you willing to let God do anything necessary to bring you to total surrender so that he is free to accomplish all that he wants to do for you and all he wants to make out of you?" I wonder what your response might be.

To have God's very best, we must be willing to submit our all to him.

Our submission will mean our growth, and that growth is a process—one that includes setbacks, failures, hard lessons, and, yes, brokenness. Our growth includes not only spiritual growth but also the renewal of our minds and emotions.

Again and again, we find ourselves being broken so that our old nature might be chipped away or a rough spot in our character might be sanded smooth.

The process is painful and difficult.

Nevertheless, it is good.

Brokenness is not something to be shunned or avoided at all costs. Rather, it is something we are to face with faith. If we truly want to be all that God designed us to be, and therefore all that God desires for us to be, we must submit to him during times of brokenness and allow him to reveal to us why we are going through this hard season and what he wants us to learn.

A PERFECT VESSEL

God declared long ago, "Like clay in the hand of the potter, so are you in my hand" (Jeremiah 18:6).

God is at work in our lives, shaping and making us into the people he longs for us to be, so that we might bring glory to him and be of maximum use to him in the building of his kingdom.

Which would you rather be? A vessel of your own design, based on your finite mind and limited creativity, power, and wisdom; a vessel of limited use and fading value? Or a vessel of God's design, based on his infinite wisdom, love, and power; a vessel of unlimited use and eternal value?

In choosing to be fashioned by God, we inevitably must choose to yield to brokenness and to allow God to remake us and renew us as he desires. And that will mean suffering, pain, hardship, and trials.

CHAPTER 2

GOD WANTS THE
BEST FOR US

Often when tragedies strike or hard times engulf us, we ask, "Where's God?"

In asking this question, we make the assumption that God must not have known what was about to befall us or else, if he were powerful enough, he would have prevented it. Or we assume that God must not love us, because surely if he loved us, he would keep us from all hurtful times and hard experiences.

We might think that, but none of that is the truth.

This is the truth: God knows. God is powerful. And God loves.

BLAMELESS, UPRIGHT, AND BROKEN

When we experience difficult times or feel great inner pain and turmoil, we usually try to assign blame. We say either, "The devil caused this" or "God caused this."

The greater likelihood is this: the devil caused it, and God allowed it.

Consider the Old Testament story of Job, who was described as being "blameless and upright; he feared God and shunned evil" (Job 1:1). Yet God gave Satan permission to "strike everything [Job] has" (v. 11), but not Job himself.

God allowed Job to suffer incredible loss for reasons that were God's alone. Throughout Job's pain and losses, however, God never abandoned Job for even a moment. He knew at each step of the way how greatly

Job was being afflicted. And our sovereign God was overseeing this refining of Job.

The good news for us anytime we find ourselves being broken is this: our sovereign God is overseeing the refining process in our lives. He sees the beginning and the end. He has a good future designed for us, and ultimately heaven awaits.

We can be sure that our period of brokenness is not the end, but rather, a passage and a process to a rich, new beginning.

Yes, God knows. God is powerful. And God loves.

GOD ALWAYS ACTS OUT OF LOVE

The motivation behind everything God does in our lives and everything he allows to enter our lives is love.

God is never acting in anger or wrath when he breaks us. Rather, God moves in our lives because he loves us too much to see us continue in our sin, remain in a lukewarm spiritual state, or go unfulfilled in his purposes for our lives. God moves in our lives so that we might change, grow, and become both spiritually mature and whole in spirit, mind, and body.

CHASTISEMENT VERSUS PUNISHMENT

God's love prompts him to chastise us when necessary. Chastisement is God's method of disciplining us. God's purpose is to lead us to confront, remove, or change those habits, attitudes, and beliefs that keep us from growing into the full stature of Christ's likeness.

Punishment is for unbelievers. It is an expression of God's wrath against those who have rejected the only Sin-bearer who can save a sinful person from that wrath. Our holy God cannot tolerate sin. He must eradicate it from his presence. The unbeliever is in an awesome, terrible position—totally exposed to God's wrath.

Punishment flows from God's wrath; chastisement flows from God's love. And God loves us so much that he longs for us to reflect his very nature and, literally, to be the body of Christ on the earth today. The chastisement we experience is a means of refinement: just as refining removes the dross and impurities from metal, so God strips us of the sin and the faults that keep us from being made whole.

GOD DOES NOT WANT TO BREAK OUR SPIRITS

God's purpose is not to break our spirits, but rather— and for our good—to break the stubbornness of our wills. He does this so he might effect his will in our lives.

A good parent knows that a child's streak of stubbornness and pride must be broken. The breaking of a child's stubbornness is not done to break the child's spirit, but rather, to help the child grow up to be a productive, law-abiding, generous, and loving spouse, friend, parent, citizen, and member of the body of Christ.

Just as a parent breaks a child's stubborn pride and willful disobedience, so God seeks to break within us the pride and disobedience that keep us from being loving, generous, Christlike people.

GOD DOES NOT DELIGHT
IN CAUSING US PAIN

Just as it is not God's desire to break our spirits, neither is it God's purpose to cause us pain.

Our heavenly Father, the sovereign God, has a purpose in allowing bad things to happen, and his purpose extends not only to my life alone or yours alone, but to the lives of many people whom you and I may influence and help.

If we believe Romans 8:28 to be true, we must believe it to be true for all circumstances in our lives: "We know that in all things God works for the good of those who love him, who have been called according to his purpose." Whatever it is that we may experience and however we may be broken, God has a good end for us. We must never limit God's ability to redeem even the worst, most pain-filled experience in our lives and turn it into something worthwhile, something that is good for us and that glorifies him.

Regardless of the source of our pain, we must accept that God knows, God is powerful, God loves, and God

is at work. We may not be responsible for what has happened to us, but we are responsible for our response to it. We must ask ourselves, "How can I walk through this pain? How can I benefit or profit spiritually from this?"

GOD'S DESIGN

Where is God? He was with you at your first taste of pain, he has been with you in the darkness, he continues to be with you, and he will be with you as he uses this experience to do his refining work in your life.

So ask God to reveal to you what he is doing in your life—and what he desires to do for you, in you, and through you as the result of your brokenness.

Ask him to help you see your brokenness in light of his great design for your life.

CHAPTER 3

WHY WE ARE BROKEN

A young man once said to me, "Sometimes I wonder why I had to go through such awful experiences before I came to the Lord. I was an alcoholic. I used people and loved things rather than loving people and using things. I got in trouble with the law and came very close to killing a couple of people because I had an accident while driving under the influence. I wish God had saved me a whole lot sooner."

I said to him, "Perhaps something in you had to die first."

He thought about that for a moment. "Yeah, you're right. I wasn't ready to give up what I called the 'good life.' I thought I had a great life until that car accident."

Before any of us can fully live as God has created us to live, we first must die to our desire to control our own lives and to live according to our plan and will.

SOMETHING HAS TO DIE
FOR LIFE TO BEGIN

Jesus said, "Very truly I tell you, unless a kernel of wheat falls to the ground and dies, it remains only a single seed. But if it dies, it produces many seeds" (John 12:24).

A single seed will never stop being just a single seed until it is dropped into the earth and covered with soil: the seed has to be buried; it has to be positioned to die with the purpose of reproducing life. Before long, the seed's outer shell breaks, and a little green sprout begins to push its way up through the soil, until eventually it breaks through into the sunshine. The seed itself disappears as a stalk of grain grows. The head of the wheat holds dozens of grains that could grow into a plant of its own. From one grain of wheat, a person could eventually plant a million acres of wheat.

Jesus was teaching that as long as the grain remains alone—unplanted and unyielded—it cannot bear fruit. He was describing, of course, what was about to happen to him: his crucifixion and his resurrection. As long as Jesus remained alive, a few people might be healed, a few might benefit from his miracles, a few might turn to God by his teaching and preaching, but ultimately, the world would remain unforgiven.

Before his life could be extended and multiplied, Jesus had to die, and he was willing to die. In turn,

he calls upon each of us to take up our cross—
sacrificially dying to ourselves and giving ourselves
to his cause—in order that we might live for him and
according to his purposes.

We must be willing to die to our affections, dreams,
desires, ambitions, and goals. We must break ourselves
of our intense love of self. We must be totally willing
for the Lord Jesus Christ to have his way in our lives.
Only then can we truly know life to the fullest and
find our purpose in life realized completely. We must
die to self in order to become more of ourselves and
eternally ourselves.

And why does God require that something be put to
death in order for it to be made alive? The fullness of
God's reasons is known only to God.

But we can see that this principle holds true
throughout his creation. We have bread only because
somebody has crushed the grain into flour. We have
salvation because Jesus allowed himself to be crushed
by the weight of your sin and mine. We have fully
productive and useful lives only because God has
crushed our self-will.

GOD WANTS TO DESIGN OUR FUTURE

Is it wrong to like quality things or to purchase the best you are able to afford? Is it wrong to desire a spouse and children? Is it wrong to want to succeed in your work?

No! What is wrong is when we feel we can't live without these things. What is wrong is substituting the acquisition of things, relationships, and accomplishments for a relationship with God. When we set our eyes on the accomplishment of our goals, we nearly always lose sight of God's goals for us. Only when we make our relationship with God our number one priority can God bring us into a position where we can achieve and receive what will truly satisfy us.

If there's anything in our lives that we think we just can't live without, that should be a warning sign to us to reevaluate our relationship with God and to take another look at our priorities.

God knows what you need. He knows what is best for you. If we turn to God, he will satisfy all of our longings for the future with perfect fulfillment. If we are willing to give up defining our own future, he'll give us something better than we could ever arrange, manipulate, or create. His best will be ours, but only if we are willing to die to our selfish independent streak and submit our lives completely to him.

GOD WANTS TO SET OUR GOALS

It's not wrong for us to set goals. What's wrong is when we set goals apart from asking God what his goals for us might be. We must always approach our goal setting with earnest prayer, asking, "What is it, God, that you desire for me to do and say and be?"

Our prayer must be the same as the one that Jesus prayed in the Garden of Gethsemane: "Not as I will, but as you will" (Matthew 26:39).

WE ARE CHRIST'S WORKMANSHIP

The Bible tells us that once we have accepted Jesus Christ as Savior, we do not own ourselves, and we do not govern or determine our own future.

We are God's workmanship, from start to finish. God leads and guides us into the good works that we are to do for him—works that are totally in keeping with the talents, skills, experiences, and abilities he has given us.

Christ Jesus is the author and finisher of our lives (see Hebrews 12:2 KJV).

As long we insist on writing our own stories, he cannot write his living will onto our hearts.

As long as we insist on forging our own paths, he cannot lead us into his paths of righteousness.

As long as we insist on governing our own lives, he cannot be our sovereign King and Lord.

As long as we insist on living life according to our own desires, he cannot impart his desires or guide us into his wholeness, fruitfulness, and blessings.

As long as we feel that we are in control of our fates, we cannot experience fully the destinies he has for us.

We are his workmanship. When we act otherwise, we are breaching our trust relationship with God and refusing to submit our lives fully to him.

CHAPTER 4

OBSTACLES TO ACCEPTING

OUR BROKENNESS

Although it's not often talked about as such, and it's really not talked about enough in Christian circles, brokenness is part of God's plan.

Brokenness clearly is part of life in this fallen world. Look at today's headlines. Google statistics about abortion, divorce, and suicide. These things don't surprise God. Jesus even promised his followers, "In this world you will have trouble" (John 16:33). But our redeemer God takes the brokenness in our lives and uses it to accomplish what has always been his plan: to humble us, invite us, and sometimes even compel us to yield our lives and hearts to him, so that he can make us more like Jesus.

Brokenness is both a fact of life and a tool in God's hands. Yet few of us readily embrace our brokenness. Several obstacles keep us from acknowledging our brokenness and letting God use it in our lives, for our good and his glory.

THE OBSTACLE OF SELF-SUFFICIENCY

Being a Christian isn't a matter of doing (going to church, singing hymns, praying, giving money, reading the Bible, sharing our faith) or not doing (smoking, drinking, swearing, sleeping around). Being a Christian is a matter of being in a relationship with Christ Jesus. The work to be done is his: Jesus is responsible for transforming us and making us more like him. He is our Author and Editor, the One who is transforming our hearts and our lives so that we grow in Christlikeness and walk according to God's plan for us.

You and I can't change our sinful nature, but God uses our brokenness to move us to a point where we acknowledge, "I can't do it by myself." Only the Holy Spirit, sent by Christ to dwell within us, can cleanse and change a human heart. Only the Holy Spirit can guide our decision making so that we will make Christlike choices.

May we let go of our illusion of self-sufficiency and accept that we are the clay, and God is the Potter.

THE OBSTACLE OF TALENTS AND GIFTS

Through the years I have seen that the most gifted people, the most self-confident, those who have the most going for them have the most difficult time yielding to God's breaking process.

The trouble with gifts and talents is not in having them, but in relying on them and trusting in them.

Those who are satisfied with what they have rarely look to God to supply them with what they truly need.

They don't—they *can't*—know what they're missing because they don't feel that they are missing anything.

Even when they hear the gospel, the highly gifted may not realize that they will never lose if they surrender their all to God. We can never lose in giving ourselves away, in living with Jesus as our Lord.

Furthermore, what we give to God, he gives back to us in greater abundance. We find in him renewal, joy, peace, and fulfillment. We simply cannot out-give God.

Neither can we do more with our lives than God can do with our lives.

THE OBSTACLE OF MISPLACED TRUST

God longs for us to trust him completely, but he leaves the choice to us. As long as we trust anything within ourselves, we aren't trusting him fully. The thing that we trust—consciously or unconsciously—instead of

God becomes a stumbling block, a barrier, a hindrance, an obstacle to our trust in God.

Self

First and foremost, we too easily trust ourselves. We are born with a proud independence. Many people post "Keep out" on the walls of their souls. Others will say, "God, you can have this percentage of my life, but this one area I reserve for myself." If we are to have the fullness of God's power, wisdom, and love, we must trust him completely, and we must reserve no part of ourselves for ourselves.

Wealth

We also readily trust in money and material assets. Too many of us can place our security in money: we find ourselves focusing more on business and less on family and church relationships. In one case I witnessed, God didn't let up until this particular man finally came to the place where he said, "God, I'm yours. I've been trusting in money all my life. Now I am choosing to trust you."

The greater miracle in the man's life was that he no longer cared about being fabulously wealthy. His identity was no longer tied up in money.

Image and Appearance

Her appearance was always very important to her. She enjoyed nice clothes, was always meticulously dressed, and never had a hair out of place.

In her seventies, though, she became ill with a degenerative disease. As her outer body wasted away, she could no longer trust in her image or appearance. She instead trusted in God, and her inner spirit began to shine in a wonderful way. She became an inspiration to every person who visited her because she shared so fully the grace of God at work in her life.

This woman died in peace, with a great joy in her heart.

Accomplishments and Reputation

Some people find security and confidence in their accomplishments and the solid reputation that resulted. But one such man found himself forced out of the

company he had founded, and he hit rock bottom. That's when he yielded to the breaking process and surrendered his life to God.

Anytime we seek to rest on our laurels, we are in danger of being broken. We are trusting in our own past performances rather than in God's provision for the present and future.

THE OBSTACLE OF WANTING TO MAINTAIN CONTROL

What area of your life are you withholding from God today? Those areas that we keep off limits to God are the very ones he focuses on so that every aspect of our independence is stripped away from us. His desire and purpose for us—for our good—is total dependence on him. When we act independently, we put ourselves in danger.

If that kind of breaking sounds severe, consider what happens in the breaking of a horse. Contrary to what many people believe, a horse's spirit isn't broken.

A well-broken horse remains strong, intelligent, and eager, and he loves to gallop when given free rein. Rather than his spirit, it is the horse's independence that is broken. A broken horse has learned immediate obedience.

Similarly, when a child of God is broken, God does not destroy his or her spirit. We don't lose our zest for living when we come to Christ. We don't lose the force of our personalities. Rather, we lose our independence.

God doesn't strip us of our free wills either, but brokenness is the condition whereby our wills are brought into full submission to God's will so that when he speaks, we put up no argument, make no rationalization, offer no excuses, and assign no blame. Instead, we immediately obey the leading of the Holy Spirit. The end result is blessing.

THE OBSTACLE OF SELF

Again, for our good, our heavenly Father is after our self-will, self-reliance, self-dependence, and self-sufficiency. He is after everything in us that smacks of self and of willful independence. For some, self is all tied up with social status—with, for instance, power, position, authority, intellectual prowess, a vibrant personality, beauty, fitness, possessions, or living in the "right" neighborhood.

God, however, wants our concept of self totally and completely grounded in his love. Getting to that point can be hard. The more we cling to whatever we are trusting instead of trusting God, the harder the breaking period may be. At times, it seems as if God must wrench from us those things that we trust more than we trust him.

Why are we afraid to let go? Because we don't want to lose control. And that is pride in its rawest form.

We are afraid that God won't love us enough to meet our needs, fulfill our desires, or give us contentment. We fear that we will go through life lacking something vital, missing out on something good, or not experiencing something we want to experience.

If we believe that God doesn't love us—or that he

doesn't love us enough—then our tendency will of course be to not trust him. Trust issues are inevitably love issues. Ask yourself today:

- Would God rob me of anything that was for my eternal good?
- Would God break in me anything that would cause me not to become the person he wants me to be?
- Would God take away from me anything that would bless me spiritually?
- Would God deprive me of anything that would build me up, edify me, strengthen me, and build my character?
- Would God steal from me anything that would bring me contentment, peace, and joy?

The answer to all these questions is a definitive, absolute NO!

At all times, in every situation and circumstance, God is at work in some area of your life, bringing you to the place where you will want to become and

achieve what he wants you to become and achieve. He is fashioning your heart to desire what he wants for you. He is working within your spirit so that you may know his will and be eager to do it. And that divine goal is why the Lord acts anytime he finds something within us that must be broken—even shattered—in order for us to become who he created us to be.

THE OBSTACLE OF OUR RESPONSE

We decide the outcome of our brokenness. We can choose to respond to brokenness with anger, bitterness, and hate.

The way to blessing, however, lies in turning to God to heal us and make us whole. We decide whether we will yield to him and trust him.

Wholeness is God's intended outcome for our brokenness. When we are whole, we can be fruitful. And when we are fruitful, we find fulfillment, peace, and joy in our lives.

CHAPTER 5

WHAT DOES IT MEAN
TO BE MADE WHOLE?

When many people think of wholeness, they automatically turn to matters of health, sickness, injury, or death. Wholeness in this discussion, though, is a matter of harmony between body, soul, and spirit. We experience wholeness when the different aspects of our lives are working together in a healthy, sound, and resilient way.

When God breaks us, he does so with the purpose of putting us back together again better than before and, ultimately, so that we might be whole.

WHOLENESS INVOLVES ALL OF OUR BEING

Let me share several key principles about wholeness.

First, we must recognize that we have three aspects to our being: body, soul, and spirit.

The body is the way in which we relate to our environment. We have five senses: we smell, see, taste, hear, and touch. We live in a physical shell that allows us to interact with the physical world.

We each have a soul comprised of our mind, will, emotions, conscience, and consciousness. The soul is our means of relating to other people. We choose with our will and mind how we will act in the world and toward other people.

We each also have a spirit. That is our inner person. With our spirit we relate to almighty God, and that truth helps us understand what happened in the garden.

Adam and Eve ate the only thing God had forbidden them to eat, and they died. But their bodies didn't die immediately in that act of disobedience. The two remained alive for hundreds of years after being sent out of the garden. Neither did their souls die: they still related to each other and to their children. What died in Adam and Eve was their capacity to relate to God spiritually.

Our sinful state—as theirs was—is a state of inner death. We may do very well in the physical realm and in the soul realm, but unless we are in right relationship with God through Jesus Christ, we are dead in the spirit realm. Only a believer in Jesus Christ has the potential to be a whole person, because unless the spirit is made alive in Christ, that person's spirit is out of sync with the rest of his or her being. To be whole we each must have a cleansed spirit, a blessing that enables us to be in relationship with God.

The Bible says that when we receive Jesus Christ as our personal Savior, the Holy Spirit comes to dwell in us. Our spirits come to life, and because of the Holy Spirit within us, we are able to enter into a living relationship with God. We are able to talk to him, and we have a new sensitivity to his voice when he talks to us. We are able in new ways to understand the Word of God and to receive guidance from the Holy Spirit. We also are more sensitive to our sin and to the Spirit's convicting power. Our spirits have been born anew. We have a new spiritual life!

The unbelieving world doesn't understand our spiritual life because the world lives by its senses and appetites. All of us—believers and nonbelievers alike—have appetites: we have a need for love, a desire to grow, a longing to learn. We have an appetite for independence. So as long as a person is without a relationship to God, these appetites degenerate into what the Bible calls the "lusts" of the flesh. But the Holy Spirit puts all of the appetites, desires, and impulses of our flesh and our souls under the command of our spirits.

For the Lord to bring us to wholeness, he must deal with the areas of our lives that keep us from wholeness. Those areas separate us from the fullness of what God desires for us.

WHOLENESS IS MORE THAN SKIN-DEEP

When we begin to see life the way God sees it, we realize that life has an ever-flowing spiritual undercurrent. All of life flows from the spiritual dimension. Our desires and ideas and emotions are motivated by the spirit and flow through the soul for expression through the body. Every act of relating to others—what we say, what we do, who we see, and why—has a spiritual dimension and purpose. In fact, everything we do in the physical, mental, or emotional realm has a spiritual component to it.

But when we regard our own brokenness, our natural tendency is to look only on the surface. We limit our perspective on brokenness to the physical or emotional realm.

The more important matters to consider in times of brokenness are these:

- What is happening in the spiritual area of my life?
- What might God want to do in my relationship with him?
- How might God work in this time of brokenness to restore me, renew me, remake me, and remold my relationship with him?
- How might God work in and through these circumstances to bring me to greater wholeness?

These questions bring us squarely back to the purpose of God: he wants to develop in us a total trust relationship with him so he might use us as whole men and women, strong in spirit, completely obedient to him, and subject to his leading.

God's purpose is always accomplished ultimately at the spiritual level.

Our role in times of brokenness is to submit not only to what God desires to do in our lives but also to his timetable. Wholeness may not come quickly or easily, but it is worth the wait.

WHOLENESS TAKES TIME

When we find ourselves broken, we need to choose to believe that God will reveal his plan and purpose to us step-by-step. We need to answer his call to trust him day by day by day. Consider Paul's words:

> We do not lose heart. Though outwardly we are wasting away, yet inwardly we are being renewed day by day. For our light and momentary troubles are achieving for us an eternal glory that far outweighs them all. So we fix our eyes not on what is seen, but on what is unseen, since what is seen is temporary, but what is unseen is eternal. (2 Corinthians 4:16–18)

It may very well seem to us that we are wasting away daily, but if we will look beneath the surface to the inner work God is doing, we are actually growing and being strengthened.

I've seen this happen countless times, very often as people struggle with terminal diseases. Their outer bodies literally seem to waste away, yet if they choose to turn to God, submit completely to him, and trust him with their lives, both an inner beauty and a spiritual strength develop that far outweigh anything happening in the physical realm.

Paul told the Corinthians to fix their eyes on what is unseen. And that is good advice for us when we are broken.

WHOLENESS GLORIFIES GOD

In eternity, you and I will be God's trophies—the trophies of his grace; the trophies of Christ's death, burial, and resurrection; the trophies of the Holy Spirit's work in our lives. Our purpose is to bring him glory.

We often lose sight of the fact that this life is preparation for the life to come. It is a process of becoming. Too often only when our wills are saddle-busted completely, do we belong—heart, soul, mind, body, spirit, and everything—to him. When that happens, your life and mine are totally and completely his responsibility. I am the Lord God's, to do with as he pleases. And that, my friend, is when the excitement in life truly begins!

CHAPTER 6

THE DEVELOPMENT OF SPIRITUAL MATURITY

We call movement along the path from where we are to where God wants us to be—in a position of total surrender to him and total wholeness—spiritual growth. The goal is spiritual maturity: God breaks us to mature us.

Spiritual growth has three aspects: change, growth, and brokenness.

CHANGE

If we are not willing to change, not willing to
grow, then we will not grow spiritually. We can't
hold on to old ways, old ideas, old feelings, or old
erroneous concepts about God, the Holy Spirit, or the
Christian life.

GROWTH

Not all change results in growth, but certainly all
growth is marked by change. Spiritual maturity means
growing up until we are fully Christlike in all of our
decisions, thoughts, feelings, and actions.

The environment necessary for growth toward
spiritual maturity is love. We grow spiritually as we
love one another.

Our growth does not move us toward independence.
That's a pattern in the natural, physical world: children
grow up to live independently of their parents.
Spiritual growth, though, is marked by increasing

dependence on the Lord Jesus Christ. Ultimate spiritual maturity is a state of total dependence on the Holy Spirit to govern, guide, and guard our lives.

BROKENNESS

A third aspect of spiritual growth is brokenness. If we are to change and grow, we must be willing to move away from what has been holding us back, pushing us down, or keeping us from being in a position to receive God's best. We must be willing to give up our hold on the things to which we have been clinging with all our might. This often requires being broken.

THE BREAKING OF MOSES

God's hand was on Moses from the day he was born into a Jewish family enslaved in Egypt. To quell the growth of the Hebrew nation lest they turn against Egypt at some point, the Pharaoh had commanded that all male Hebrew babies die. Baby Moses, however, was protected in a basket floating on the Nile, adopted by one of Pharaoh's daughters, nursed by his own mother and taught the things of God, and later raised in the seat of Egyptian government. But Moses never forgot his Hebrew roots, and one day he killed an Egyptian who had been beating a Hebrew. When Moses realized that his crime had been witnessed, he immediately fled to Midian. For forty long years, Moses worked for his father-in-law, Jethro, as a shepherd in the desert (Exodus 1–2).

Moses went from Pharaoh's palace, where he lived like a son of Pharaoh, to being an exile and a lowly shepherd in the desert. Surely Moses was being broken because Moses needed to be changed. God needed to take Moses from a position of self-reliance to a position of total reliance upon him.

In addition, Moses—like the Hebrew people as a whole—had been Egyptianized. They had adopted much of the Egyptian culture and had even begun to worship the gods of Egypt. After all, they had lived in Egypt for four hundred years by the time Moses came on the scene.

God had to deal with the Egyptianization of Moses so that when God delivered his people from Egypt, God alone would be glorified, and God alone would receive the credit. Then, and only then, could the

Hebrews begin to see that they must put their trust solely in God. God's purpose in breaking Moses was with a much larger intent of breaking the Israelites so that he might refashion them once again to be his people.

A STRIPPING AWAY OF EVERYTHING NOT OF GOD

You may be thinking, *Does God do this to everybody he plans to use?* God does follow this same principle in breaking each one of us for his use and his purposes. God's purpose in our lives is not to make us famous, prominent, prestigious, or wealthy. His purpose in our lives is to bring us to the position of absolute nothingness so that we will recognize that all we have of value in this life is God and God alone.

The man Moses used to be and the man he was at the end of forty years in the desert no doubt seemed like two different people to Moses.

And that was the point. The Moses whom God sent back to Pharaoh to lead the Hebrews out of Egypt was not the man who had fled from Pharaoh.

BROKENNESS IS COUNTERCULTURAL

So much of brokenness goes against what we are taught in our culture. We are taught to be self-confident, to make our plans and set our goals, to refuse to move or budge from our purposes. In the desert, Moses had to learn to be God-reliant, to let God set the agenda for his life, and to do whatever God asked him to do.

Jesus, of course, is the epitome of reliance upon God. Jesus lived out God's plan. And that is what God desired for Moses. It's also what God desires for you and me.

Someone once said, "A soul is converted in a moment of time, but to become a saint takes a lifetime." Conversion happens instantly; maturity takes many years.

By God's grace, we finally strip ourselves of all self and say, "All that I am and all that I have is God's. He is in me and I am in him, and that's all that matters."

THE PROCESS OF SPIRITUAL MATURITY IN YOUR LIFE

So what is God stripping away from your life?

What comes to mind when you think of being broken?

What have you put between you and total surrender to God? What do you trust more than you trust God? What do you love more than you love God?

Every person I know has an intuitive understanding of what God desires to remove from their lives. We can usually identify what we are afraid to do without or what we most fear we will lose.

Still, no matter how long it takes or how difficult the process may be for us, God will break us . . . change us . . . and cause us to grow until we reach spiritual maturity.

PREPARATION FOR
SUPERNATURAL MINISTRY

Each one of us has a ministry. God has specific opportunities to serve designed for us, places where we can fully use our God-given talents, gifts, and skills. He has placed us in a unique time, in the places he has chosen for us, and among specific people to accomplish his ministry. That's why he grows us spiritually: so that we might minister to others with depth, spontaneity, and gracious generosity.

God caused Moses to mature spiritually so he could liberate the Hebrew people from bondage and lead them to a land where they could live in the fullness of God's promises to them. He gave Moses a supernatural ministry. And we too are called to supernatural ministry.

You may have noted that I use the word *supernatural* to describe ministry. That's because if ministry is real, it must be supernatural: it must be

God-inspired and God-empowered. *Ministry* means
"service." Anybody can minister to another person's
needs. But for a person to be engaged in supernatural
ministry means that he or she ministers to others
under the direction of God and by the power of his
Holy Spirit.

Running your business according to biblical
principles, raising a godly family, teaching school,
working in a hospital—any number of activities can be
done as a supernatural ministry as long as we do it for
God's glory and as long as we invite the Holy Spirit to
work through us.

Several aspects of supernatural ministry are
important to note.

SUPERNATURAL MINISTRY
HAS AN OBJECTIVE

God told Moses, "I want you to go to Pharaoh and tell
him to let my people go." This was the clearly stated
objective of Moses' ministry.

SUPERNATURAL MINISTRY
REQUIRES ACTIVE TRUST

Hudson Taylor, founder of the China Inland Mission, expressed God's perspective well: "The work is mine and mine alone; thy work—to rest in me."

SUPERNATURAL MINISTRY IS
EMPOWERED BY GOD

Imagine how Moses must have felt when he heard God's ministry assignment. Go into Pharaoh's court and demand that he let all of the slaves go? Organize nearly three million people to leave the only home they've ever known to go to a land they've never visited? God's objective for Moses' ministry was vast and complicated.

Know that whatever supernatural ministry God calls you to, it will undoubtedly seem monumental to you. That's part of God's plan. He wants us to rely on him totally for the accomplishment of his objective.

If we could do the ministry in our own strength and according to our own wisdom, we wouldn't need God, and the ministry wouldn't be supernatural.

So God sent Moses to Pharaoh with only one thing—a shepherd's staff. That staff was a symbol of God's presence with his chosen people. Moses brought nothing to the task: he had been reduced to a position of total trust in God.

And God came through. Again and again. Moses didn't convince Pharaoh. He didn't open the Red Sea. He didn't provide food. He didn't provide water. He didn't map out the route through the wilderness. God did. Moses only had to obey what God told him to do.

Ministry inevitably follows that pattern. We may plant the seed of God's truth. But God grows it. We may provide bandages and medicines. But God does the healing. We may pray earnestly. But God does the miracle. We do our part, and God does the part that only God can do.

So anytime God calls us to supernatural ministry, he reminds us, "I'm the one who will accomplish the task. You do what I tell you to do, and I will make it happen." The provision and the power for accomplishing what God calls us to do are his and his alone.

SUPERNATURAL MINISTRY
AFFECTS OTHERS

Only God could mature Moses spiritually. The same held true for the Israelites as a group. Only God could de-Egyptianize his people. Toward that end, he gave them the law, led them through the wilderness, protected them from their enemies, and fed them with manna. God invaded every area of their lives—breaking them and rebreaking them—so these people he had chosen as his own would be different from everyone around them.

By breaking the Hebrews, God separated them from all the pagan, adulterous people around them just as he had separated Moses. God called his people to a different set of customs, a different mode of dress, a different ritual of worship, a different pattern of behavior. God gave them their own economy, their own lifestyle, and their own set of commandments and laws. He further commanded the Israelites not to intermarry or have fellowship with those who didn't serve him, the one true and living God.

And why did God want to bring his people to spiritual maturity? Again, for supernatural ministry. God had told Abraham that through his family, all the nations of the world would come to know God.

This huge objective came with a promise: "If you do what I tell you to do—if you are totally obedient to me—I will bless you and make you a blessing."

God's purpose for breaking you and bringing you to a place of wholeness and spiritual maturity is so that he will be able to use you as his tool in bringing others to wholeness and spiritual maturity.

God teaches, comforts, and encourages us so that we might teach, comfort, and encourage others.

He gives us spiritual gifts and financial prosperity so that we might help others and introduce them to Jesus.

SUPERNATURAL MINISTRY REQUIRES TOTAL SACRIFICE

Broken people arrive at a place of total self-sacrifice, and that position is critical to our ability to minister.

We can't have supernatural ministry at work in our lives if we aren't willing to totally give our love, time, compassion, gifts, and prayers.

We must be willing to roll up our sleeves and get dirty.

We must be willing to work and sacrifice.

We must be willing to suffer on behalf of others.

We can't grow to spiritual maturity without suffering and pain, and we can't engage in supernatural ministry without being willing to endure even more suffering and pain.

You and I cannot be effective in the supernatural ministry God calls us to if we do not remain fully yielded to him. God does not bring us to supernatural ministry so that we can do that ministry on our own, striving to accomplish great things on our own strength. Instead, God calls us to continue to surrender our lives to him, day by day, experience by experience, year by year. We must remain in that position of total surrender and commitment.

Broken, made whole, brought to a degree of spiritual maturity yet still growing, we serve where

God calls, and we discover a sense of fantastic, indescribable, awesome purpose and meaning. We are here so that God might use us to bring glory to himself! We are here so that God might call us into paths of supernatural ministry that will bring about the accomplishment of his plan for all humankind. We are here to be blessed by God so that we might be a blessing to others

But first, you and I must be willing to be broken, to change, to grow. Before God can use us mightily, he must know that we are completely surrendered to him.

CHAPTER 7

THE PROCESS OF BREAKING

From God's perspective, our being broken is a very systematic process, but we experience pain, confusion, and disorientation—the chaos of brokenness. God does have a plan for each of us, though. He works through circumstances to accomplish his purposes, and he never loses control of the breaking process, as the life of the apostle Peter illustrates.

Peter—called Simon when Jesus first met him—was a fisherman, impulsive, strong-willed, and outspoken. Why did Jesus choose a fellow like Peter? For the same reason God chooses you and me: he sees all we can be.

Like all of us, Peter needed to be broken so that he might be made usable for kingdom work and yielded to God's will. Jesus was willing to engage in that process in Peter's life. In fact, the breaking process Jesus oversaw changed Simon the reed into Peter the rock.

GOD TARGETS THE AREA

God targets the areas in our character that need to be broken, and the areas are the same in all of us.

- Strengths and Weaknesses: God often targets what we see as a strength in our lives. Why? Because we are much less prone to submit our strengths to him. That's because we think, *I can handle this on my own!* We fail to turn to God and seek his help or allow him to lead us.
- Attitudes, Habits, and Relationships: If any of these are contrary to what God desires for us, they are subject to being broken. For example,

God will always confront idolatry, greed, addictions, and racial prejudice.

- Desires: If we have a strong desire for something, to the point where we cling to it and consider it even more valuable than our relationship with God, this desire is subject to being broken. God is jealous for our affection, our love, our time, and our desire. He wants to be the number one priority in our lives, and he will break anything that will damage our relationship with him.

What was your response to the statement "God is jealous"? Does that sound like our holy, perfect God has a sinful flaw? He doesn't, and a couple definitions will help here. *Jealousy* is our ardent desire to possess and protect something that is rightfully ours. *Envy* is the desire for possessions or relationships that are *not* rightfully ours. So since God is our Creator and we rightfully belong to him, he is appropriately jealous of anyone and anything that attempts to woo us away from him and to take his place as our top priority.

God wants us to completely rely on him. So God crushes, breaks, shatters, and removes anything from our lives—very often something dear to us that we are holding too tightly—that either separates us from his love, forms a barrier between him and us, or hinders our ability to serve our Lord.

Jesus saw severe hindrances in Peter's life.

- Jesus knew that Peter's impetuous, volatile nature could be controlled by intense faith or intense fear. When, at Jesus' invitation, Peter got out of the boat and started walking on the stormy seas, he became filled with fear when he took his eyes off his Lord (see Matthew 14:22–30). Jesus needed to break the hold that fear had on Peter if he was to follow Jesus without wavering .

- Jesus knew that he must break in Peter that desire to have things go his way rather than God's way. When Jesus stated that he would suffer and be killed in Jerusalem, Peter objected to that happening. Peter was objecting to God's plan for salvation (see Matthew 16:21–23).

- Jesus knew that he needed to break Peter's smug self-righteousness. Remember that Peter was the one who asked how many times he should forgive his brother, magnanimously offering seven times. Jesus clarified: seventy times seven (see Matthew 18:21–22 KJV). Jesus wanted Peter to be unendingly generous with God's forgiveness.

- Jesus knew that he needed to break Peter's pride, evident when Peter declared that he would never do the awful deed that Jesus had prophesied. Peter was absolutely sure that he would not deny knowing Jesus three times before the rooster crowed at dawn. Thinking that he was above what Jesus had prophesied, Peter proclaimed that he would even die for his Lord. Instead, he spoke the three denials that Jesus had foretold. And the rooster crowed (see Matthew 26:31–35).

- Jesus knew that he needed to teach Peter that the kingdom of God is not to be established by force, but by the power of love alone. Remember in Gethsemane when the crowd came to arrest

Jesus? Peter had brought along a sword and cut off the right ear of the high priest's slave (see Luke 22:50–51). Jesus healed the man's ear, and Peter saw that love, not force, would be the way in Jesus' kingdom.

Again and again, Peter was broken. Bit by bit, in situation after situation, Jesus worked to pulverize the disciple's pride, egotism, and self-sufficiency.

And God will do no less in our lives. He will target the areas that keep us from trusting him completely and yielding to him fully.

GOD ARRANGES THE CIRCUMSTANCES

Just as the target area for God breaking us is subject to his will, so are the circumstances that lead to our being broken. God choreographs the situations that will cause us to confront exactly what he desires to change in our lives. At other times, God will simply allow us to follow the pathway of sin that we have chosen. He

will give us enough rope so we can entangle ourselves. With either approach, we eventually come to the place where we are forced to say, "Okay, God. I'll do it your way."

GOD CHOOSES THE TOOLS

In addition to targeting the area that needs to be broken and arranging the circumstances for that breaking, God chooses the tools.

God has used hurtful remarks, false accusations, people manipulating situations for their own benefit, and great challenges that initially seemed overwhelming or potentially devastating.

We don't choose the tools God uses; he chooses. Just as we can't tell God *when* to break us, we can't tell him *how* to break us. The selection of methods is his business. But I can tell you this with a fair degree of certainty: the tool will be sharp, painful, and unavoidable, and loss is virtually always a part of being broken. Through it all, may we pray, "God, I'm yours. No matter what happens to me, I am going to trust you."

OUR BROKENNESS AFFECTS OTHERS

Before we look at a couple of tools God uses, let's acknowledge that when he breaks us, our brokenness affects the people around us. (Similarly, God's breaking process in the lives of others may affect us.) Whatever the impact our brokenness has on the people around us, know that God will use the situation to refine and grow them. They, for instance, will have an opportunity to face the state of their spiritual maturity, lack of wholeness, or lack of trust in God. Nothing is ever wasted in the breaking process.

OUR ENEMIES AS TOOLS

Sometimes God will use our enemies to persecute us or to keep the pressure on us until he has our full attention and full compliance. We pray against the assault from our enemies, and in response, God often doesn't deal with our enemies as much as he deals with us. Thankfully, God reveals rather quickly what he desires us to learn, do, or change. Then, as soon as we come to grips with what God is seeking to break in us, our enemies cease to be a problem.

OUR FAMILY AS TOOLS

The family is one of the foremost crucibles that God uses to grind away those traits in us that are unlike Christ Jesus. Our spouses and our children can truly be tools that humble us and refine us.

GOD CONTROLS THE PRESSURE

Just as God chooses the target, sets up the circumstances, and selects the tools for our brokenness, so he controls the amount of pressure we are under.

He knows exactly how much pressure is enough to break us (the amount varies from person to person). In other words, God sets limits on our brokenness. Our brokenness ends when our wills are broken and we yield to God in submission. Our brokenness also ends when its intensity will damage God's purpose for our lives. God will not allow you or me to be broken or shattered to the point where we cannot serve in the supernatural ministry he has prepared for us.

RESISTANCE PROLONGS THE PROCESS

As implied above, our resistance to God's breaking process will prolong it, and our willingness to yield to the Lord will shorten it. This is the only aspect of the breaking process we can impact; we don't choose the targets, dictate the circumstances, or choose the tools. But our response to the testing is our way of impacting its duration. So the earlier we identify what God is doing in our lives and yield to it, the better it is for us. When we resist the breaking process, God must turn

the vise a little tighter, chisel a little deeper, and sand a
little longer.

BROKEN BUT NOT DESTROYED

God's purpose is to break our wills, not our spirits.
His purpose is not to destroy us, but to bring us to
a position of maximum wholeness, maturity, and
usefulness in his kingdom. He wants us to yield control
of our lives to him.

Like Peter, each one of us has a very difficult time
giving up control. But God uses brokenness to bring
us to the point where we have nothing to say except,
"Lord Jesus, what would you have me do?"

God makes no mistakes in the breaking process. He
knows precisely what areas to target in our lives. He
knows what circumstances will be effective and what
tools to use. And he knows how much pressure we can
take. Our loving God is all about the task of perfecting
us, for our good and his glory.

CHAPTER 8

OUR PROTEST AGAINST BROKENNESS

Many people today believe they can run away from God, resist his claim on their lives, escape his wrath, and live their own way.

All of us have times when we don't want to give up our way, don't want to yield, don't want to have our wills broken by God. This rebellious streak in us resents and resists God, and we realize that we are not all that different from the prophet Jonah.

HOW CAN WE RUN FROM GOD?

Consider the futility of trying to run from God.
How do you run from the presence of our infinite
God, who is everywhere all the time? Everything
that is—everybody who is alive, every place in the
universe—exists in his presence. Yet nearly always
when God wants to break us, we seek a means of
escaping what he desires for us to be and do. In fact,
sometimes in our rebellion we say, "Lord, I know
what you're telling me to do, but I have a better way."
Unless we willingly choose to obey God explicitly and
immediately, we are in rebellion.

YOUR REBELLION BRINGS AN IMMEDIATE RESPONSE

God responds immediately to our acts of rebellion.
Sometimes he responds by sending a storm into
our lives. That is exactly what he did in the life of
Jonah.

God called Jonah to preach the saving message "Repent!" to his enemies in Nineveh—and Jonah boarded a boat heading in the opposite direction. When the storm hit, Jonah knew why, and he told the frightened sailors to throw him overboard. Fear overcame their reluctance, they threw Jonah into the ocean, the sea got calm, and a big fish swallowed the runaway prophet.

At the end of three days and three nights in that great fish, Jonah prayed to the Lord, and his was the prayer of a man yielding to brokenness. Jonah finally submitted his will completely to God, and he went to Nineveh to preach. Unlike Jonah, however, the Ninevites responded quickly to God's breaking process. They repented immediately.

And they repented even though Jonah didn't cry out God's words in love, compassion, and mercy. Jonah was simply obedient. He yielded his will to God, but not his attitude. Jonah didn't really want to see the people converted. His words were right, but his motive was wrong. And Jonah's attitude got worse after he saw the widespread repentance.

We have no indication that Jonah had any further ministry. God apparently could not use Jonah until he submitted his heart as well as his will to the Lord's plans. And Jonah refused to yield.

In what condition are your heart and your will today? Are you yielded to God so that he can use you in his kingdom work? If not, know that God desires to change your will and your attitude.

THE THREE CALLS OF GOD ON EVERY PERSON'S LIFE

God issues at least three calls to every person.

First is the call to salvation and repentance: God invites us to accept by faith that Jesus Christ's shed blood at Calvary was the all-sufficient, substitutionary, atoning death that brings about the forgiveness of our sins.

Second is the call to sanctification or separation. God desires us to live so totally committed to him that sin no longer reigns in our lives. This is a call to allow the power of the Holy Spirit living within us to guide our lives and help us resist temptation.

Third, God issues a call to service. This call may be to serve him within the home, in the business world, in the mission field, in places needing volunteers, or in any number of other arenas. God's call to service is always highly personal and very specific to a person's talents, abilities, gifts, and willingness to be used by him for his purposes.

Some people rebel against the call to salvation. Some people rebel against the call to sanctification. Some people resist God's call to service or to supernatural ministry. They hear God say to them, "I want you to do this," and they respond, "I know what you said, but I think I'll do this first [or instead]."

Those who rebel against God's call to specific service never find true satisfaction or a feeling of fulfillment in the lives they choose for themselves. Rebellion brings no happiness; it brings only sorrow, depression, anger, bitterness, and frustration.

Once God calls you to do something, nothing you offer as a substitute has any value.

THE ROOTS OF REBELLION

Our rebellion against God has several roots:

Pride: Whenever you and I choose to do something our own way and rebel against God's call, we are saying, "I know better than you know, God."

Fear: Ask yourself, "Why am I resisting what God is asking me to do, to give up, or to change?" What do you fear?

Force of Will: Do you have so much self-determination, persistence, and self-confidence that you will continue to rebel no matter how intense the pressure?

Force of Mind: Rather than yield to God, do you work harder on developing a Plan B as God applies greater pressure?

God wants us to face our rebellious spirit, turn from it, and say to him, "I can't figure out life on my own. I can't manipulate my way to genuine joy, hope, and fulfillment. I need you *in* my life, God, and *in charge of* my life."

ATTEMPTING TO DOWNPLAY REBELLION

We find all kinds of ways to justify our decisions, don't we? At times we blame others for the brokenness we are experiencing. Other times we blame circumstances, past or present. We may rationalize, run, or rebel. In fact, our blaming and rationalizing are sure signs that we are resisting brokenness and are in rebellion.

The right response is to confess, "I am in rebellion against God." The sooner we reach that conclusion and face that reality, the sooner we can experience God's resolution of our brokenness.

THE HIGH COST OF REBELLION

Think of the price Jonah paid for his rebellion. He lost his family, his job, his income, and his assets. He lived with a guilty conscience: he knew he was disobeying God. Jonah also put himself in a position of being out of fellowship with God. And the prophet created emotional bondage for himself with his anger, hatred, and bitterness.

When we exercise our free will and rebel as Jonah did, God eventually says to us, "All right. You win, but you lose." God will shelve us in the very state we have chosen for ourselves.

If we have chosen not to accept God's call to salvation, we remain unsaved, lost.

If we have chosen not to accept God's call to sanctification, we will continue to struggle against temptation and the consequences of poor choices, bad decisions, and sin.

If we have chosen not to accept God's call to service, we remain unfulfilled, struggling to find genuine meaning and purpose for our lives.

Rebellion puts an end to our growth. It robs us of wholeness. It cuts off our ability to mature spiritually.

PRAYING FOR THE PERSON
WHO IS IN REBELLION

When we sense that a person is in rebellion, our prayer should be, "God, send that person enough trouble so he [or she] will turn to you." Ask God to use circumstances to break that individual's will and bring him or her to the point of surrendering to him. This prayer is a prayer for that person's ultimate good.

Sometimes people ask me to pray that God might remove certain situations from their lives. Instead, I

pray that these people will yield themselves to God and his purposes, that God will uphold and strengthen them in those circumstances, and that they will come through these circumstances spiritually stronger and more mature than before. Rather than pray for escape, we pray for God's grace to be at work so they can face this situation with both courage and the ability to fully trust God to work this situation for their good and his glory.

MISSING OUT ON THE BLESSING

Rebellion ultimately causes us to miss out on the blessings God desires for us. If we aren't walking with the Lord, we may know a little happiness, a little love, a little joy in this life, but we will never know the fullness of joy, God's unconditional love, or the hope of eternal life with our Lord and Savior. Resistance to God also keeps us from experiencing his power, wisdom, and presence. It keeps us from his blessings.

CHAPTER 9

PREPARATION TO BEAR MUCH FRUIT

Who is God?

We can answer that question many ways: he is Creator, Lord, the Almighty, our heavenly Father, or the Man upstairs. In John 15:1, Jesus called himself "the true vine, and my Father is the gardener." And the Son and the Father are working to grow fruit in their people, in you and me.

Scripture speaks of both inner fruit—qualities of character—and outer fruit—the works we do that bring glory to God and extend his kingdom.

THE INNER FRUIT OF THE HOLY SPIRIT

The inner fruit we are to bear is produced in us by the Holy Spirit as we remain faithful to the Lord Jesus, as we abide in the vine. We can only acquire this inner fruit by walking closely with the Lord in obedience each day.

God's Work in Us

God is at the center of the universe; we are not. He requires that we serve him. He is not our errand boy. He is the Lord God Almighty. We are highly presumptuous when we demand that he do our bidding. The proper relationship with God is one in which we put ourselves in a position to do his bidding.

When we do not seek the presence of God within us as much as we desire the things that we want God to do for us, we are not worshiping God. We are worshiping God's provision; we are worshiping material things.

Giving Up Our Idols

Idolatry can take subtle forms as we place too much value on certain possessions or relationships. Oh, we can give up the thing, the activity, the relationship we know God has asked us to give up, yet not give up that thing, activity, or relationship in our hearts. If God has asked you to give up something, give it up. Give it up literally *and* give it up in your heart.

God Is Our All in All

Brokenness brings us to the place where we say, "All that matters is God and his presence in my life," the place where we awaken with God's purposes in mind, praying, "What do you want me to do, say, and be today in order to bring you glory?" At that point we are in submission: we desire God to produce in us the inner fruit of Christlike character.

The Character of Christ

The fruits of the Spirit described by the apostle Paul in Galatians 5:22–23 ESV and listed here reflect the character of Jesus Christ. His character is marked by these:

- *Love*: Christlike sacrificial love gives, and then gives more, and then gives still more. When we are following Christ and his example, we can pour out this kind of love on others.
- *Joy*: Every time we are broken by God and sin is defeated in our lives, joy is the outcome. And when we are full of joy, people notice and are drawn to the Lord, the source of our joy.
- *Peace*: When we submit our lives completely to Christ, we choose to trust that he is in control, and we are able to rest in his arms. Being at peace in one's spirit is a countercultural and appealing trait in this pressure-filled world.
- *Patience*: When we know that we are God's for all eternity, we are much more inclined to wait on him for what he has for us in this life, and we can be patient with others who we think are interfering with our plans.
- *Kindness*: Brokenness brings us to the place where we realize we have no rights; we have turned them over to God. We no longer insist on having our own way or getting what we want

when we want it. As a result, we are kinder to others.

- *Goodness*: When God breaks us, we realize that God alone is good and that the only goodness we have in us is because the Holy Spirit lives in us. The Spirit's presence in us gives us the desire to do good works, make good decisions, and come up with good solutions. The goodness of God also compels us to look for the good in others and to encourage them, to help those in need, to pray for those who don't know the Lord, and to seek justice on behalf of those who are oppressed.

- *Faithfulness*: A broken spirit enables us to say, "I am truly yours, Lord. You alone are God, and I never want to stray." The Holy Spirit produces in us a desire to be in close relationship with the Father and to never leave him, not for a moment. In human relationships, our faithfulness may be evident in our integrity and being true to our word.

- *Gentleness*: We are able to be gracious and gentle with others when we have experienced brokenness because we recognize that God has been gracious and gentle with us.

- *Self-control*: When we turn total control of our lives over to God, he gives us self-control, the ability to say no to Satan's temptations, and the capacity to resist evil. This self-control makes it easier for us to live in a way that honors God and respects others.

In addition to producing this fruit in us, God breaks our voracious hunger to satisfy our own longings and desires. He breaks us so we will want what he wants, and we discover that God wants us to have what we need and what will bring us joy. Brokenness changes our desires.

THE OUTER FRUIT OF GOD'S INNER PRESENCE

Brokenness causes us to consider the fruitfulness of our witness. The outer fruit that God calls us to produce is to declare his truth and to meet the needs of those we encounter who are in need. We are to be ready witnesses to God's love and power. We are to reflect God's compassion with our actions when someone needs help, with our lifestyles as unbelievers watch us, with service that builds up the body of Christ, and with our words when someone asks us about our hope, joy, or love.

Again, the reason for brokenness is so that we might realize that the life we live is not our life: it is Jesus' life. And we must surrender on a daily basis to the life that he desires to live through us.

Then, what we discover through brokenness is that when we truly submit our will to Jesus' will and allow him to work through us, our service to others has much greater power and effectiveness.

The way to the blessing of a new character—the character of the Lord Jesus Christ himself—and of a new power in your personal ministry and service to others is going to be a path that involves brokenness. God has no other plan for us. Brokenness is his way to blessing.

CHAPTER 10

THE PROMISE OF BLESSING

What is a blessing?

So often in our world today, *blessing* is defined as "prosperity." But a blessing is so much more.

A blessing from God is a gift that is intended for our eternal benefit or good. A genuine blessing always has an eternal component.

THE BROKENNESS AND BLESSING OF PAUL

The apostle Paul knew what it was to be broken, and he also knew what it was to experience God's blessing, especially the blessing that comes in the wake of brokenness.

No one has the insights, illumination, or inspiration that Paul had. After his encounter with God on the Damascus Road, God called Paul to years of solitude before embarking on his ministry. And those years of being alone with God—of allowing God to reveal to him the truth of Christ Jesus through the Scriptures and experience—were highly valuable years in his life.

Perhaps no other human being has gone through as much suffering, pain, and hardship as Paul did in his years of ministry, but God used those times to refine the apostle.

The two greatest truths Paul likely learned from his brokenness were these: his own limitations and God's unlimited grace. Those are the most valuable truths any of us can learn.

Our Limitations

Paul learned that he could not live the Christian life in his own strength. And God desires for each of us to come to that realization, to come to the end of ourselves, to recognize that we aren't capable of doing the good that we want to do—of living in a way that pleases God—in our own strength, knowledge, or force of personality (see Romans 7:18–25).

If we don't accept this truth, we will continue to rely on ourselves—our background and heritage, our education and degrees, our determination and ambition, our commitment and willpower. God breaks us in order to teach us that we cannot live an abundant life on this earth or an eternal life in heaven without his help.

God's Unlimited Grace

Paul also learned that when he was at his very weakest, the power of God was released through him in its greatest intensity.

Paul stayed in touch with his weakness because of a thorn "in [the] flesh" (2 Corinthians 12:7–10). Whatever that thorn was, it made Paul feel insufficient and weak. It acted in Paul's life as a tool of brokenness.

He accepted it as God's way of bringing him to the blessing of knowing that God was sufficient for him regardless of any outer circumstances.

This truth about the unlimited nature of God's grace is very likely a lesson we only learn when we are brought to the absolute limits of our own endurance and ability to experience pain and suffering. God knows precisely how much heat we can take in his process of refining us to perfection.

The refining of precious metals—especially silver and gold—begins at low heats. Certain impurities respond quickly to heat, and they rise to the surface of the metal and are skimmed away. The heat is then increased. Other impurities rise to the top of the cauldron of molten metal and are skimmed off. Only under extremely intense heat will the most stubborn of impurities separate from the metal and rise to the top where they can be removed.

The process is the same in our lives. The breaking in our lives is by degrees. God breaks us layer by layer, bit by bit. If God moved immediately to the deepest areas of our lives, we couldn't stand it. We'd be so overwhelmed that not only would our wills be broken, but our very spirits would be shattered.

The most deeply embedded things within us are subject to the greatest amount of brokenness. Only when these deep-seated, strongly entrenched weaknesses or flaws are removed can we truly say, "I know God's grace is sufficient for anything."

Paul knew the full intensity of God's refining fire in his life. And from those experiences he gained an understanding of God's unlimited grace.

FIVE GREAT BLESSINGS FROM BROKENNESS

At least five great blessings come from our being broken.

The Blessing of Understanding God Better

As we are broken, we understand the absolutes of God—that his commandments are exact, his promises are sure, his methods and his timetable are entirely his own, and his provision is complete.

We understand the Scriptures more fully. We see patterns of how God works in human lives. We have a deeper understanding of God's love. We know more fully what it means to be accepted by God on the basis of nothing in ourselves, but solely because he is a loving Father. We understand more fully the purpose of the cross. We grow in understanding God's patience and love and kindness and forbearance. We have an experiential understanding of his long-suffering. We know with a growing certainty that he is in control of our lives completely and eternally.

The breaking process always lifts almighty God, the cross, and the grace of God to a higher level in our lives than we had placed those truths before. We are given a glimpse of God's glory and of his divine nature. We come to a new depth of understanding of all God's many attributes.

There is no end to what we can learn about God. This blessing is therefore an infinite one.

The Blessing of Understanding Ourselves Better

As we are broken by God, we come to a much deeper understanding of ourselves. We are able to trace the avenues, thought patterns, and trends of our lives from our childhood through our growing-up years. We can gain a new understanding of certain experiences in our past and how they affected us, for better or worse. We see our emotional flaws and discover how poorly we both show love and receive love. We face our limitations and frailties, and we see how fear has stifled us.

In our brokenness we also come to know our God-given talents, gifts, and abilities. We see ways in which the Lord has strengthened us, prepared us, and fashioned us. We also see how God has dealt with us in tenderness and mercy.

One thing we always understand very clearly in times of brokenness is that we are sinners. Brokenness always involves sin—the sin of pride and the sin of rebellion, among the other sinful behaviors God desires to remove from us. The breaking process reveals to us that we are being continually refined by God. Sin is being peeled from our lives, layer by layer.

What a wonderful blessing it is to recognize that while we still have the capacity to sin, we have been freed by Christ Jesus to denounce sin, be forgiven of it, and have victory over it!

Once we truly are broken and once we have totally submitted our lives to God, a peace floods our souls that is beyond understanding and beyond explaining (Philippians 4:7).

The Blessing of Increased Compassion for Others

Along with gaining a greater understanding of the nature of God and of ourselves through brokenness, we begin to look at other people differently. We begin to see that others are no worse and no better than we are.

We all are sinners at our core. We all are in need of God's grace and the refining power of the Holy Spirit working in our lives. We all need to change, grow, and

develop in certain ways. None of us is without flaws and weaknesses.

Through brokenness, we come to the place where we can say:

- "Father, you were patient with me. I can be patient with him."
- "Father, you showed kindness and mercy to me. I can extend kindness and mercy to her."
- "Father, you forgave me. I can forgive this person who hurt me."

Brokenness makes us less critical and judgmental. It also opens us up to new ways we can share God's love with others.

The Blessing of a Greater Zest for Life

When we come to the end of ourselves, we find that we have a greater appreciation of all God's gifts to us. Our hearts are renewed with thanksgiving and the awareness of God's goodness to us.

Our interest in life is rekindled. The hard parts of

our souls break up so that we are quicker to laugh with gusto and to cry with tenderness.

The Blessing of an Increased Awareness of God's Presence

God is with us always, but brokenness makes us more sensitive to his presence. He comforts us and assures us that he will never leave us or forsake us.

And in our brokenness, in the intimacy of our spirits, God speaks to us of his great love for us. He tells us how much he values us and desires good for us. He assures us that he is with us and is working in us.

When we feel assured of God's presence with us, we are secure, and there's no greater security. God reveals himself to us as our all-sufficiency, our total provision, our ultimate protection. That releases us from fear, pressure, and worry. It produces in us an abiding peace that cannot be described and an unspeakable joy that fills our hearts to overflowing, regardless of the circumstances.

WORTH THE STRUGGLE

When we yield to God's purposes in our lives and begin to experience the blessings that come from brokenness, we can say, "I'm thankful for this trial. Praise God it's over, but praise God that, because he loves me, he used it to refine me. I wouldn't trade the blessing of this experience for anything in the world!"

THE PURIFYING WORK OF PAIN

The hallmark of several years in my life was pain. God used it to soften me, change my thinking, and expand my compassion for others who are in pain. I wouldn't trade those changes for anything.

Some things we may not fully understand until eternity. But the perspective that God is at work keeps me from anger, bitterness, and hostility. So I have chosen that perspective.

THE CONDITION FOR BLESSING

God places only one condition on the blessings that he
has for us through brokenness: we must be willing to
submit to him.

If we are willing to surrender ourselves to him, he
leads us to total victory in the aftermath of brokenness.
It may take months or years for that victory to be
realized or recognized, but victory is assured.

But if we balk in rebellion and refuse to surrender
to God, we greatly curtail God's blessing. We place a
barrier of mistrust and rebellion between ourselves and
his outpouring of blessings into our lives.

GOD CONTINUES TO WORK IN US

God will not give up on us. He will continue to work
in us, bringing us from one experience of brokenness
to the next and blessing us along the way.

Friend, we never outgrow our need to be broken in
one way or other. And praise God for that! He loves

us so much that he never gives up on us, never loses interest in us, and never rejects us. He asks only that we trust him to be our God, so that we might be his people and bring him glory.

MY PRAYER FOR YOU

Father, how loving, how tender, how gentle, how gracious, how good are your methods for bringing us ever closer to you so that we might experience more fully your love and care for us.

Help us cast away those things that are contrary to your purposes for us. Help us embrace those things that you call us to be and to do.

We desire more of you in our lives. We desire to know you better, to have a deeper relationship with you, and to feel your abiding presence in our lives always.

Break us, dear Father, so that you might mold us into the image and likeness of your Son, our Savior, in whose name we pray, amen.